THE BOOKS OF
KAHLIL GIBRAN

"His power came from some great reservoir of spiritual life else it could not have been so universal and so potent, but the majesty and beauty of the language with which he clothed it were all his own."   CLAUDE BRAGDON

∴

Beloved Prophet
The Love Letters of
Kahlil Gibran and Mary Haskell
Edited by Virginia Hilu

This Man from Lebanon—
A Study of Kahlil Gibran
by Barbara Young

PUBLISHED BY ALFRED A. KNOPF

NYMPHS

OF THE VALLEY

NYMPHS
OF THE VALLEY

BY

KAHLIL GIBRAN

Translated from the Arabic by
H. M. NAHMAD

1981

NEW YORK : ALFRED·A·KNOPF

CONTENTS

THE FOUR ILLUSTRATIONS

IN THIS VOLUME

ARE REPRODUCED FROM

ORIGINAL DRAWINGS BY

THE AUTHOR

MARTHA

MARTHA

Her father died whilst she was still in the cradle, and her mother before she was ten years old. She was left an orphan in the house of a poor neighbor who lived with his wife and children and existed on the fruits of the soil in a small isolated hamlet amidst the beautiful valleys of Lebanon.

Her father died and bequeathed to her nothing save his name and a poor hut standing among the nut trees and poplars. From her mother she inherited only tears of grief and her orphan state. She sojourned a stranger in the land of her birth; alone among the intertwining trees and towering rocks. Each morning she walked barefooted in a tattered dress behind a milch cow to a part of the valley where the pasture was rich, and sat in the shade of a tree. She sang with the birds and wept with the brook while she envied the cow its abundance of food. She looked at the flowers and watched the fluttering butterflies. When the sun sank below the horizon and hunger overtook her she returned to the hut and sat beside her guardian's daughter and ate greedily of the maize bread with a little dried fruit and beans dipped in vinegar and olive oil. After the meal she spread some dry straw on the ground and laid herself down, her head resting on her arms. She slept and sighed, wishing that life were one long deep sleep undisturbed by dreams or awakening. At the approach of dawn her guardian roused her roughly to attend to his needs and she awoke from her slumbers afraid and trembling at his harshness and anger. Thus passed the years for Martha, the unfortunate, amongst those distant hills and valleys.

Soon she began to feel in her heart the stirring of emotions she had never before known; it was like becoming aware of the perfume in the heart of a flower. Dreams and strange thoughts crowded upon her like a flock that comes across a watercourse. She became a woman, and she likened herself in some vague manner to fresh virgin soil that is yet to be planted with the seeds of knowledge and feel upon it the imprints of experience. A girl profound and pure of soul whom a decree of fate had exiled to that farmstead where life passed through its appointed phases with the seasons of the year. It was as though she were a shadow of an unknown god residing between the earth and the sun.

Those of us who have spent the greater part of our existence in crowded cities know little of the life of the inhabitants of the villages and hamlets tucked away in Lebanon. We are carried along on the current of modern civilization. We have forgotten — or so we tell ourselves — the philosophy of that beautiful and simple life of purity and spiritual cleanliness. If we turned and looked we would see it smiling in the spring; drowsing with the summer sun; harvesting in the autumn, and in the winter at rest; like our mother Nature in all her moods. We are richer in material wealth than those villagers; but their spirit is a nobler spirit than ours. We sow much but reap nothing. But what they sow they also reap. We are the slaves of our appetites; they, the children of their contentment. We drink the cup of life, a liquid clouded with bitterness, despair, fear, weariness. They drink of it clear.

Martha reached the age of sixteen years. Her soul was a polished mirror reflecting all the loveliness of the fields, and her heart was like the wide valleys which threw back voices in echo.

One autumn day when nature seemed filled with sadness she sat by a spring, freed from its earthly prison like thoughts from the imagination of a poet, looking at the fluttering of yellowed leaves as they fell from the trees. She watched the wind playing with them as Death plays with the souls of men. She gazed on the flowers and saw that they were withered and their hearts dried up and broken into little pieces. They were storing their seeds in the earth as women their trinkets and jewelry during times of war and disturbance.

While she sat thus looking at the flowers and trees and sharing with them their pain at the passing of summer, she heard the sounds of hoofs on the broken stones of the valley. She turned round and beheld a horseman riding

6

slowly toward her; his bearing and dress told of ease and wealth. He dismounted from his horse and greeted her gently, in a manner no man had ever used to her before.

"I have strayed from the road leading down to the coast. Could you direct me to it?" he asked.

She stood upright by the edge of the spring, straight like a young branch, and answered him: "I do not know, my master, but I will go and ask my guardian; for he knows." She uttered these words, at the same time feeling a little afraid, with a shyness and modesty that heightened her tenderness and beauty. She was about to go when the man stopped her. The red wine of his youth coursed strongly through his veins. His look toward her changed as he said: "No, do not go." She remained standing and wondering, for she felt in his voice a force that prevented her from movement. She stole a glance at him. He was looking at her carefully; a look whose meaning she could not understand. Then he smiled at her in so bewitching a manner as to make her want to weep at its very sweetness.

He let his eye rest with affection on her bare feet, her pretty wrists, her smooth neck, her soft thick hair. He noted, with a rising passion, her gleaming skin given her by the sun, and her arms, which nature had made strong. But she stayed silent and ashamed. She did not want to go away, nor, for reasons she was unable to divine, could she find power to speak.

The milch cow returned that evening to the enclosure without her mistress; for Martha did not go back. When her guardian came home from the fields, he sought her in all the hollows but did not find her. He called her by name but there came no answer save echoes from the cave and the soughing of the wind in the trees. He returned sorrowing to his hut and told his wife. She wept silently throughout that night, saying within herself: "I have seen her in a dream in the claws of a wild beast, who tore her body to pieces the while she smiled and wept."

That is what I gleaned of the life of Martha in that pretty hamlet. I learned it of an old villager who had known her since the days of her childhood. She had disappeared from those places leaving nothing behind her save a few tears in the eyes of the guardian's woman, and a pathetic memory that rode on the morning breeze over the valley and then, like the breath of a child on a windowpane, faded.

II

I returned to Beirut in the autumn of 1900
after having passed my college vacation in
North Lebanon. Before returning to my studies
I spent a week wandering around in the town
with some of my fellow students, savoring with
them the delights of freedom, for which youth
hungers and which is denied it at home and
within the four walls of a classroom. It is like a
bird that, finding its cage door open, flies to and
fro, its heart swelling with song and the joy of
escape.

Youth is a beautiful dream, but its sweetness
is enslaved by the dullness of books and its
awakening is a harsh one.

Shall there come a day when wise men are
able to unite the dreams of youth and the delights of learning as reproach brings together
hearts in conflict? Shall there come a day when

man's teacher is nature, and humanity is his book and life his school? Will that day be?

We know not, but we feel the urgency that moves us ever upwards toward a spiritual progress, and that progress is an understanding of the beauty of all creation through the kindness of ourselves and the dissemination of happiness through our love of that beauty.

That evening as I sat in the porch of my lodgings watching the moving crowds and listening to the cries of the street venders, each extolling the excellence of his wares and foods, a boy came up to me. He was about five years of age and clad in rags and tatters, and on his shoulder he carried a tray filled with bunches of flowers. In a voice broken and feeble, as though handed down to him as a heritage of long suffering, he asked me to buy a flower from him.

I looked into his small pale face and remarked his eyes, dark with the shadows of weariness and poverty; his mouth, open a little like a wound in a scarred breast; his emaciated bare arms and his puny little body bent over the tray of flowers like a rose-plant yellowed and

withered among fresh green plants. I saw all
these things as it were at one glance, and in my
pity I smiled, a smile in which was something
of tears. Those smiles that break forth from the
depths of our hearts and rise to our lips. Should
we heed them not, they find outlet through our
eyes.

I bought some of his flowers, but it was his
speech that I wished to buy, for I felt that behind his wistful looks was curtained off the act
of a tragedy — a tragedy of the poor, playing
perpetually upon the stage of the days. An act
seldom seen because it is a tragedy. When I spoke
to him with kind words, he grew friendly as
though having found a body in whom he could
seek protection and safety. He gazed at me in
wonder, for he and his like are accustomed only
to rough words from those other boys who look
upon boys of the streets as things defiled and of
no account and not as little souls wounded by
the arrows of fortune. I then asked him his
name.

"Fouad," he answered, with his eyes averted
to the ground.

"The son of whom, and where are your people?"

"I am the son of Martha, woman of Ban."

"And your father?" I asked.

He shook his small head as one who knows not what a father is.

"Then where is your mother, Fouad?"

"At home, ill."

These few words from the boy's lips smote my ears, and out of them my inmost feelings fashioned strange and melancholy forms and figures for I knew, at once, that the unfortunate Martha whose story I had heard from the villager was now ill in Beirut. That girl who yesterday was among the trees and valleys away from harm was today suffering the harshness of hunger and pain in a city. The orphan girl who passed the days of her childhood with nature, tending her cows in the beautiful fields, had been carried away on the tide of corrupt civilization to become a prey in the grasp of misery and misfortune.

As these things passed through my mind the boy continued to gaze at me as though he saw

with the eye of his innocent spirit my broken
heart.

He made as if to go away but I seized his
hand and said: "Take me to your mother; I
want to see her."

He led the way, walking before me silent
and wondering. From time to time he looked
back to see if in truth I was following behind
him. With feelings of fear and dread I walked
on through dirty streets wherein the air was
leavened with the breath of death, past tumble-
down houses wherein evil men practiced their
evil deeds behind the curtains of night. Through
winding alleyways that twisted and writhed like
vipers I walked behind that boy of tender years
and innocent heart and unvoiced courage. The
courage of those acquainted with the wiles and
tricks of the dregs in the midst of a city known
to the East as the "Bride of Syria" and the
pearl in the crown of kings. We reached the
outskirts of the quarter at last, and the boy entered a mean dwelling to which the passage of
years had left only a crumbling side.

I went in after him, my heart beating rap-
idly as I approached the room. I found myself

14

in the middle of a room the air of which was damp. It possessed no furniture save a lamp whose feeble light cut the gloom with its yellow rays, and a couch whose appearance spoke of dire poverty and destitution and want. Upon the couch was a sleeping woman with her face turned to the wall as though taking refuge in it from the cruelties of the world; or mayhap seeing in its stones a heart more tender and compassionate than the hearts of men. The boy went up to her crying: "Mother, Mother." She turned round and saw him pointing at me. At this she made a movement beneath the tattered bed-coverings and, in a voice rendered bitter by the sufferings of a spirit in agony, cried:

"What do you want, O man? Do you come to purchase the last shreds of my life so that you might defile it with your lust? Go from me, for the streets are filled with women ready to sell their bodies and souls cheaply. But I, I have naught for sale save a few gasps of breath, and those will Death soon buy with the peace of the grave."

I moved near to the bed. Her words moved me to the depths of my heart for they were the epitome or her tale of sorrow. I spoke to her and wished that my feelings might flow with my words.

"Be not afraid of me, Martha. I come not to you as a ravening beast but as a sorrowing man. I am of Lebanon and long have I dwelt in the midst of those valleys and villages by the forest of the cedars. Fear not, then, Martha."

She listened to my words and knew in her being that they rose from the deepnesses of a spirit that wept with her, for she shook and trembled upon her bed like a naked branch before the winter wind. She put her hands over her face as though she would hide herself from that memory, frightening in its sweetness, bitter in its beauty. After a silence in which was a sighing her face reappeared between her trembling shoulders. I saw her sunken eyes gaze at an unseen thing standing in the emptiness of the room, and her dry lips quiver with the quiver of despair. In her throat the approach of death rattled and with it a deep and broken moaning. Then she spoke. Entreaty and supplication gave her utterance, and weakness and pain brought back her voice:

"You have come here from kindness and compassion, and if pity for the sinful be deemed a pious deed, and compassion on those who have gone astray a meritorious act, then shall Heaven reward you for me. I pray you go from here and return whence you come, for your presence in this place will earn for you shame, and your pity for me will bring insult and contempt upon you. Go, go ere anybody see you in this foul room, filthy with the filth of swine. Walk swiftly and cover your face with your cloak so that no passer-by may know you. The compassion that fills you will not bring back my purity, neither will it wipe out my sin, nor stay the strong hand of Death from me. My wretchedness and guilt have banished me to these dark depths. Let not your pity bring you near to blemish. I am a leper dwelling amidst graves. Do not approach me lest people hold you unclean and draw away from you. Return now, but mention not my name in those sacred valleys, for the shepherd will deny the diseased lamb in fear for his flock. If you should make mention of me say that Martha, woman of Ban, is dead; say naught else."

She then took her son's two small hands and kissed them sadly. She sighed and spoke again:

"People will look upon my child with contempt and a mocking, saying this one is the offshoot of sin; this is the son of Martha, the harlot; this is the child of shame, of chance. They will say of him more than that, for they are blind and will not see and know not that his mother has purified his childhood with her agony and tears and atoned for his life with her sorrow and misfortune. I shall die leaving him an orphan among the children of the streets, alone in this pitiless existence, bequeathing to him naught save a terrible memory. If he be a coward and a weakling, he will be ashamed before this memory; if he be courageous and just, then will his blood be stirred. If Heaven should perchance preserve him and let him grow to be a man in strength, then will he be helped by Heaven against those who have wronged him and his mother. If he should die and be delivered from the snare of years, he shall find me beyond, where all is light and rest, awaiting his coming."

My heart inspired me to speak:

18

"You are no leper, Martha, even if you dwelt among graves. You are not unclean even if life has put you in the hands of the unclean. The dross of the flesh cannot reach out its hand to the pure spirit, and the masses of snow cannot kill the living seeds. What is this life except a threshing-floor of sorrows upon which the sheaves of souls are trodden ere giving up their yield? But woe to those ears that are left without the threshing-floor, for the ants of the earth shall carry them away and the birds of the sky shall take them up and they shall not enter into the storehouses of the master of the field.

"You are oppressed, Martha, and he who has oppressed you is a child of the palaces, great of wealth and little of soul. You are persecuted and despised, but it were better that a person should be the oppressed than that he should be the oppressor; and fitter that he should be a victim to the frailty of human instincts than that he should be powerful and crush the flowers of life and disfigure the beauties of feeling with his desire. The soul is a link in the divine chain. The fiery heat may twist and distort this link and destroy the beauty of its roundness, but

it cannot transmute its gold to another metal;
rather will it become even more glittering. But
woe to the bruised and the weak when the fire
shall consume him and make him ashes to be
blown by the winds and scattered over the face
of the desert! Ay, Martha, you are a flower
crushed beneath the feet of the animal that is
concealed in a human being. Heavy-shod feet
have trodden you down, but they have not destroyed that fragrance which goes up with the
widow's lament and the orphan's cry and the
poor man's sigh toward Heaven, the fount of
justice and mercy. Take comfort, Martha, in
that you are the flower crushed and not the foot
that has crushed it."

She listened with intentness as I spoke, and
her face was lighted up with solace as the clouds
are illuminated by the soft rays of the setting
sun. She motioned me to sit beside her. I did
so, seeking to learn from her eloquent features
of the hidden things of her sad spirit. She had
the look of one who knows that he is about to
die. It was the look of a girl yet in the springtime of life who felt the footfalls of Death by
her broken-down bed. The look of a woman

forsaken who yesteryear stood in the beautiful valleys of Lebanon filled with life and strength, but now exhausted and awaiting deliverance from the bonds of existence.

After a moving silence she gathered together the remnants of her strength. She started to speak, her tears adding meaning to the words, her very soul in every breath she took:

"Yes, I am oppressed. I am the prey to the animal in men. I am a flower trodden underfoot. . . . I was sitting by the edge of the spring as he rode by. He spoke kindly to me and said that I was beautiful, that he loved me and would not forsake me. He said that the wide spaces were places of desolation and the valleys the abode of birds and jackals. . . . He took me and drew me to his breast and kissed me. Until then I knew not the taste of kisses, for I was an orphan and outcast. He mounted me behind him on the back of his horse and took me to a fine house standing alone. There he gave me garments of silk and perfumes and rich food and drink. . . . All this did he do, smiling, and behind soft words and loving gestures did he conceal his lust and animal desires. After he had satisfied himself of my body and brought low my spirit in humility he went away, leaving inside me a living flame fed by my liver, and it grew in swiftness. Then I went out into this darkness from between the embers of pain and the bitterness of weeping. . . . So was life cut into two parts; one weak and grieving, and the other small and crying into the silences of the night, seeking return to the vast emptiness. In that lonely house my oppressor left me and my suckling child to endure the cruelties of hunger and cold and aloneness. No companion had we save fear and haunting; neither had we helper save weeping and lament. His friends came to learn of my place and know of my need and weakness. They came to me, one following upon another. They wanted to buy me with wealth and give me bread against my honor. . . . Ah, many times did my own hand determine to set free my spirit. But I turned from that, for my life belonged not to me alone; my child had part in it. My child, whom Heaven had thrust aside from it into this life as it had exiled me from life and cast me into the depths of the abyss. . . . Behold now, the hour is at

22

hand and my bridegroom Death is come after long absence to lead me to his soft bed."

After a deep silence that was like the presence of spirits in flight, she lifted up eyes veiled by the shadows of death and in a gentle voice said:

"O Justice who are hidden, concealed behind these terrifying images, you, and you alone, hear the cry of my departing spirit and the call of my neglected heart. You alone do I pray and beseech to have mercy on me and guard with your right hand my child and with your left receive my spirit."

Her strength ebbed and her sighing grew weak. She looked toward her son with grief and tenderness, then lowered her eyes slowly and in a voice that was almost a silence recited:

"Our Father which art in heaven, hallowed be Thy name. . . . Thy kingdom come. Thy will be done on earth as it is in heaven. . . . Forgive us our transgressions. . . ."

Her voice ceased, but her lips still moved for a while. When they grew still, all movement left her body. A shudder ran through

her and she sighed and her face became pale.
Her spirit departed and her eyes remained gaz-
ing at the unseen.

With the coming of dawn Martha's body
was laid in a wooden coffin and carried on the
shoulders of two poor persons. We buried her
in a deserted field far out from the town, for
the priests would not pray over her remains,
neither would they let her bones rest in the
cemetery, wherein the cross stood guard over
the graves. No mourners went to that distant
burial-ground save her son and another boy
whom the adversities of existence had taught
compassion.

DUST OF THE AGES
AND THE
ETERNAL FIRE

DUST OF THE AGES
AND THE ETERNAL FIRE

I

[Autumn, 116 B.C.]

The night was still and all life slept in the
City of the Sun.[1] The lamps in the houses scattered around the great temples in the midst of
olive and laurel trees had long been extin-
guished. The rising moon spilled its rays over
the whiteness of the tall marble columns which
stood upright like giant sentinels in the tranquil
night over the shrines of the gods. They looked
in wonder and awe toward the towers of Lebanon, dwelling in rugged places on distant
heights.

---

[1] I.e., Baalbek, city of Baal, the sun god. The ancients
knew it as Heliopolis; it was one of the loveliest cities of
Syria, and its ruins still stand.

At that magic hour poised between the spirits of the sleeping and dreams of the infinite, Nathan, son of the priest, entered the temple of Astarte.[1] He carried in his trembling hand a torch and kindled with it the lamps and the censers. The sweet smell of frankincense and myrrh rose in the air, and the image of the goddess was adorned with a delicate veil like the veil of desire and longing that enshrines the human heart. He prostrated himself before an altar overlaid with ivory and gold, raised his hands in supplication, and lifted eyes filled with tears to the heavens. In a voice strangled with grief and broken by harsh sobs, he cried:

"Mercy, O great Astarte. Mercy, O goddess of love and beauty. Have pity on me and lift the hand of death from off my beloved, whom my soul has chosen to do your will. The potions and powders of the physicians have availed nothing, and the charms of the priests and wise men are in vain. There remains but your sacred

---

[1] Goddess of love and beauty among the ancient Phœnicians, who worshipped her in Tyre, Sidon, Byblos, and Baalbek. The Greek Aphrodite and the Roman Venus.

name to help and succor me. Answer, then, my prayer; look to my contrite heart and agony of spirit, and let her that is the part of my soul live so that we may rejoice in the secrets of your love and exult in the beauty of youth, which proclaims your glory. . . . From the depths do I cry unto you, sacred Astarte. From out of the darkness of this night do I seek the protection of your mercy. . . . Hear my cry! I am your servant Nathan, son of Hiram the priest, who has dedicated his life to the service of your altar. I love a maiden and have taken her for my own, but the brides of the Jinn have breathed upon her beautiful body the breath of a strange disease. They have sent the messenger of death to lead her to their enchanted caves. He now lies like a roaring hungry beast by her couch, spreading his black wings over her and stretching out his defiled hands to wrest her from me. Because of this have I come to you. Take pity on me and let her live. She is a flower that has not lived to enjoy the summer of its life; a bird whose joyful song greeting the dawn is cut off. Save her from the clutches of death and we will sing praises and make burnt

29

offerings to the glory of your name. We will bring sacrifices to your altar and fill your vessels with wine and sweet scented oil and spread your tabernacle with roses and jasmine. We will burn incense and sweet-smelling aloe wood before your image. . . . Save her, O goddess of miracles, and let love conquer death, for you are the mistress of love and death."

He stopped speaking, weeping and sighing in his agony. Then he continued: "Alas, sacred Astarte, my dreams are shattered and the last breath of my life is fast ebbing; my heart is dying within me and my eyes are burned with tears. Sustain me through your compassion and let my beloved remain with me."

At that moment one of his slaves entered, came slowly toward him, and whispered in his ear: "She has opened her eyes, my lord, and looks around her couch but does not see you. I come to call you, for she cries for you continually."

Nathan rose and went out quickly, the slave following. On reaching his palace he entered the room of the sick girl and stood over her bed. He took her thin hand in his and kissed her lips repeatedly as though he would breathe new life into her emaciated body. She turned her face, which had been hidden among the silken pillows, toward him and opened her eyes a little. Upon her lips appeared the shadow of a smile — all that remained of life in her beautiful body; the last ray of light from a departing spirit; the echo from the cry of a heart fast approaching its end. She spoke, and her breath came in short gasps like that of a starveling child.

"The gods call me, betrothed of my soul, and Death has come to part us. . . . Grieve not, for the will of the gods is sacred and the demands of Death are just. . . . I am going now, but the twin cups of love and youth are still full in our hands and the ways of sweet life lie before us. . . . I am going, my beloved, to the meadows of the spirits, but I shall return to this world. Astarte brings back to this life the souls of lovers who have gone to the infinite before they have tasted of the delights of love and the joys of youth. . . . We shall meet again, Nathan, and together drink of the morning dew from the cups of the narcissus and re-

joice in the sun with the birds of the fields.
. . . Farewell, my beloved."

Her voice grew low and her lips began to tremble like the petals of a flower before the dawn breeze. Her lover clasped her to him, wetting her neck with his tears. When his lips touched her mouth they found it cold like ice. He gave a terrible cry, rent his garments, and threw himself upon her dead body, while his spirit in its agony hovered between the deep sea of life and the abyss of death.

In the stillness of that night the eyelids of those who slept trembled, and the women of the quarter grieved, and the souls of children were afraid, for the darkness was rent by loud cries of mourning and bitter weeping rising from the palace of Astarte's priest. When morning came the people sought Nathan to console him and soothe him in his affliction, but they did not find him.

Many days later, when the caravan from the east arrived, its leader related how he had seen Nathan far off in the wilderness wandering like a stricken soul with the gazelles of the deserts.

Centuries passed and the feet of time obliterated the work of the ages. The gods went from the land, and other gods came in their stead — gods of anger wedded to destruction and ruin. They razed the fine temple of the City of the Sun and destroyed its beautiful palaces. Its verdant gardens became dry, and drought overtook its fertile fields. Nothing remained in that valley except decaying ruins to haunt the memory with ghosts of yesterday and recall the faint echo of psalms chanted to a past glory. But the ages that pass on and sweep away the works of man cannot destroy his dreams, nor can they weaken his innermost feelings and emotions; for these endure as long as the immortal spirit. Here, perhaps, they are concealed; there they may go into hiding like the sun at eventide or the moon with the approach of the morning.

II

[Spring, A.D. 1890]

Day was waning and the light was fading as
the sun gathered up her garments from the
plains of Baalbek. Ali Al-Husaini[1] turned with
his flock toward the ruins of the temple and
sat down by the fallen pillars. They looked like
ribs of a long-forgotten soldier that had been
broken in battle and rendered naked by the elements. The sheep gathered around him brows-
ing, lulled into safety by the melodies of his
pipe.

Midnight came and the heavens cast the
seeds of the morrow into its dark depths. The
eyelids of Ali grew tired with the specters of
wakefulness. His mind became weary with the
passing of the processions of imagination
marching through the awful silence amidst the

---

[1] The Husainis are an Arab tribe dwelling in tents
around Baalbek.

34

ruined walls. He supported himself on his arm while sleep crept upon him and covered his wakefulness lightly with the folds of its veil as the fine mist touches the surface of a calm lake.

Forgotten was his earthly self as he met his spiritual self; his hidden self filled with dreams transcending the laws and teachings of men. A vision appeared before his eyes and things hidden revealed themselves to him. His spirit stood apart from the procession of time ever hurrying on toward nothingness. It stood alone before the serried ranks of thoughts and contending emotions. He knew, or he was about to know, for the first time in his life, the causes of this spiritual hunger overtaking his youth. A hunger uniting all the bitterness and sweetness in existence. A thirst bringing together a cry of yearning and the serenity of fulfillment. A longing that all the glory of this world cannot blot out nor the course of life conceal.

For the first time in his life Ali Al-Husaini felt a strange sensation awakened in him by the ruins of the temple. A feeling without form of the remembrance of incense from the censers.

A haunting feeling that played unceasingly upon his senses as the fingertips of a musician play upon the strings of his lute. A new feeling welled up from out of nothingness — or perhaps it was from something. It grew and developed until it embraced the whole of his spiritual being. It filled his soul with an ecstasy near to death in its kindness, with a pain sweet in its bitterness, agreeable in its harshness. A feeling born of the vast spaces of a minute filled with sleepiness. A minute that gave birth to the patterns of the ages as the nations grow from one seed.

Ali looked toward the ruined shrine, and his weariness gave place to an awakening of the spirit. The ruined remains of the altar appeared to his sight and the places of the fallen pillars and the foundations of the crumbling walls grew clear and sharp. His eyes became glazed and his heart beat violently, and then suddenly, as with one who was till then sightless, the light returned to his eyes and he began to see — and he thought and reflected. And out of the chaos of thought and confusion of reflection were born the phantoms of memory,

and he remembered. He remembered those pillars standing upright in greatness and pride. He recalled the silver lamps and censers surrounding the image of an awe-inspiring goddess. He recalled the venerable priests laying their offerings before an altar overlaid with ivory and gold. He recalled the maidens beating their tambourines and the youths chanting praises to the goddess of love and beauty. He remembered, and saw these figures becoming clear before his gaze. He felt the impressions of sleeping things stirring in the silences of his depths. But remembrance brings back naught save shadowy forms, which we see from the past of our lives; neither does it bring back to our ears except the echoes of voices that they once heard. What then was the link joining these haunting memories to the past life of a youth reared among the tents, who passed the springtime of his life tending his sheep in the wilderness?

Ali rose and walked among the ruins and broken stones. Those distant remembrances raised the covering of forgetfulness from his mind's eyes as a woman brushes away a cobweb

37

from the glass of her mirror. And so it was until he reached the heart of the temple and then stood still as though a magnetic attraction in the earth were drawing his feet. And then he suddenly saw before him a broken statue lying on the ground. Involuntarily he prostrated himself before it. His feelings overflowed within him like the flowing of blood from an open wound; his heartbeats rose and fell, like the rise and fall of sea waves. He was humbled in its sight and he sighed a bitter sigh and wept in his grief, for he felt an aloneness that wounded and a distance that annhilated, separating his spirit from the beautiful spirit that was by his side ere he entered this life. He felt his very essence as naught save part of a burning flame that God had separated from his self before the beginning of time. He felt the light fluttering of wings in his burning bones, and around the relaxed cells of his brain a strong and mighty love taking possession of his heart and soul. A love that revealed the hidden things of the spirit to the spirit, and by its actions separated the mind from the regions of measurement and weight. A love that we hear

38

speaking when the tongues of life are silent; that we behold standing as a pillar of fire when darkness hides all things. That love, that god, had fallen in this hour upon the spirit of Ali Al-Husaini and awakened in it feelings bitter and sweet as the sun brings forth the flowers side by side with thorns.

What thing is this love? Whence does it come? What does it want of a youth resting with his flock among the ruined shrines? What is this wine which courses through the veins of one whom maidens' glances left unmoved? What are these heavenly melodies that rise and fall upon the ears of a bedouin who heard not yet the sweet songs of women?

What thing is this love and whence does it come? What does it want of Ali, busied with his sheep and his flute away from men? Is it something sowed in his heart by man-wrought beauties without the awareness of his senses? Or is it a bright light veiled by the mist and now breaking forth to illumine the emptiness of his soul? Is it perchance a dream come in the stillness of the night to mock at him, or a truth that was and will be to the end of time?

39

Ali closed his tear-filled eyes and stretched out his hands like a beggar seeking pity. His spirit trembled within him, and out of its trembling came broken sobs in which were both whining complaint and the fire of longing. In a voice that only the faint sound of words lifted above a sigh he called:

"Who are you that are so close to my heart yet unseen by my eyes, separating myself from my self, linking my present to distant and forgotten ages? Are you a nymph, a sprite, come from the world of immortals to speak to me of the vanity of life and the frailty of the flesh? Are you mayhap the spirit of the queen of the Jinn risen from the bowels of the earth to enslave my senses and make of me a laughing-stock among the young men of my tribe? Who are you and what thing is this temptation, quickening and destroying, which has seized hold of my heart? What feelings are these that fill me with fire and light? Who am I and what is this new self I call 'I' yet which is a stranger to me? Is the spring water of life swallowed up with the particles of air and I am become an angel that sees and hears all things secret? Am I drunk of the Devil's brew and become blinded to real things?"

He fell silent for a little while. His emotion grew in strength and his spirit grew in stature. He spoke again:

"O one whom the spirit reveals and brings near and whom the night conceals and makes distant, O beautiful spirit hovering in the spaces of my dreams, you have awakened within my being feelings that were aslumber like flower seeds hidden beneath the snow, and passed as the breeze, the bearer of the breath of the fields. And touched my senses so that they are shaken and disturbed as the leaves of a tree. Let me look upon you, if you be then of body and substance. Command sleep to close my eyelids that I might see you in my dreaming, if you be free of the earth. Let me touch you; let me hear your voice. Tear aside the veil that covers my whole being and destroy the fabric that conceals my divineness. Grant me wings that I might fly after you to the regions of the assembly on high, if you be of those that inhabit there. Touch with magic my eyelids and I shall follow you to the secret places of the Jinn, if you be one of their nymphs. Put your unseen hand upon my heart and possess me, if you be free to let follow whom you will."

So did Ali whisper into the ears of darkness words moving up from the echo of a melody in the depths of his heart. Between his vision and his surroundings flowed phantoms of the night as though they were incense rising out of his hot tears. Upon the walls of the temple appeared enchanted pictures in the colors of the rainbow.

So passed the hour. He rejoiced in his tears and was glad in his grief. He listened to the beating of his heart. He looked to beyond all things as though seeing the pattern of this life slowly fading and in its place a dream wonderful in its beauties, awful in its thought-images. As a prophet who looks to the stars of the heavens watching for divine inspiration, so he awaited the comings of the minutes. His quick sighing stopped his quiet breathing and his spirit forsook him to hover around him and then return as though it were seeking among those ruins a lost loved one.

The dawn broke and the silence trembled at the passing of the breeze. The vast spaces smiled the smiles of a sleeper who has seen in his sleep the image of his beloved. The birds appeared from out of clefts in the ruined walls and moved about among the pillars, singing and calling out one to the others and heralding the approach of day. Ali rose to his feet and put his hand to his hot brow. He looked about him with dull eyes. Then like Adam when his eyes were opened by the breath of God, he looked at all before him and wondered. He approached his sheep and called them; they rose and shook themselves and trotted quietly behind him toward the green pastures.

Ali walked on before his flock, his large eyes looking into the serene atmosphere. His inmost feelings took flight from reality to reveal to him the secrets and closed things of existence; to show him that which had passed with the ages and that which yet remained, as it were in one flash; and in one flash to make him forget it all and bring back to him his yearning and longing. And he found between himself and the spirit of his spirit a veil like a veil between the eye and the light. He sighed, and with his sigh was a flame stripped from his burning heart.

He came to the brook whose babblings proclaimed the secrets of the fields, and he sat him down on its bank beneath a willow tree whose boughs hung down into the water as though they would suck up its sweetness. The sheep cropped the grass with bent heads, the morning dew gleaming on the whiteness of their wool.

After the passing of a minute Ali began to feel the swift beating of his heart and the renewed quaking of his spirit. Like a sleeper whom the sun's rays have startled into wakefulness he moved and looked about him. He beheld a girl coming out from among the trees carrying a jar upon her shoulder. Slowly she walked toward the water; her bare feet were wet with dew. When she came to the edge of the stream and bent to fill her jar she looked toward the opposite bank and her eyes met the eyes of Ali. She gave a cry and threw the jar to the ground and drew back a little. It was the act of one who finds an acquaintance who has been lost.

44

A minute passed by and its seconds were as lamps lighting the way between their two hearts; creating from the silence strange melodies to bring back to these two the echo of vague remembrances, and show to each one the other in another place, surrounded by shadows and figures, far from that stream and those trees. The one looked at the other with imploring in the eyes of each; and each one found favor in the eyes of the other; each listened to the sighing of the other with ears of love.

They communed, the one with the other, in all the tongues of the spirit. And when full understanding and knowledge possessed their two souls, Ali crossed the stream, drawn thither by an invisible power. He drew nigh to the girl, embraced her, and kissed her lips and her neck and her eyes. She made no movement in his arms, as though the sweetness of the embrace had robbed her of her will and the lightness of touch taken from her all strength. She yielded as the fragrance of the jasmine gives itself up to the currents of air. She dropped her head upon his breast like one exhausted who has found rest, and sighed deeply. A sigh telling of the birth

45

of contentment in a constricted heart and the stirring of life within that had been sleeping and was now awakened. She raised her head and looked into his eyes, the look of one who despises the speech customary among men by the side of silence — the language of the spirit; the look of one who is not content that love should be a soul in a body of words.

The two lovers walked among the willow trees, and the oneness of each was a language speaking of the oneness of both; and an ear listening in silence to the inspiration of love; and a seeing eye seeing the glory of happiness. The sheep followed them, eating the tops of flowers and herbs, and the birds met them from all sides with songs of enchantment.

When they came to the end of the valley, which time the sun had risen and cast upon the heights a golden mantle, they sat down by a rock that protected the violets with its shadow. After a time the girl looked into the black eyes of Ali while the breeze played in her hair as though it were invisible lips that would kiss her. She felt bewitched fingertips caressing her tongue and lips, and her will was a prisoner. She spoke and said in a voice of wounding sweetness:

"Astarte has brought back our souls to this life so that the delights of love and the glory of youth might not be forbidden us, my beloved."

Ali closed his eyes, for the music of her words had made clear the patterns of a dream that he saw ofttimes in his sleep. He felt that unseen wings were bearing him away from that place to a room of strange form. He was standing by the side of a couch on which lay the body of a beautiful woman whose beauty death had taken with the warmth of her lips. He cried out in his anguish at this terrible scene. Then he opened his eyes and found sitting beside him the maiden; upon her lips was a smile of love and in her glance the rays of life. His face lighted up and his spirit was refreshed, the visions were scattered, and he forgot both the past and the future. . . .

The lovers embraced and drank of the wine of kisses until they were satisfied. They slept

47

each enfolded in the arms of the other until the shade moved away and the sun's heat awakened them.

YUHANNA THE MAD

YUHANNA THE MAD

And in the summer Yuhanna went out every morning to the field leading his oxen and his calves and carrying his plow over his shoulder, the while listening to the songs of the thrushes and the rustling of the leaves in the trees. At noontide he sat beside the dancing stream that wound its way through the lowland of the green meadows, where he ate his food, leaving unfinished morsels of bread on the grass for the birds. In the evening, when the setting sun took with it the light of day, he returned to his humble dwelling, which looked out over the villages and hamlets of North Lebanon. There, as he sat with his aged parents and listened in silence to their conversation and their talk about happenings of the times, a feeling of sleepiness and restfulness gradually overtook him.

During the winter days he crouched by the fireside for warmth and listened to the soughing of the wind and the cry of the elements, pondering the way the seasons followed one upon another. He looked out of the window toward the valleys under their garment of snow, and the trees denuded of their leaves like a crowd of poor people left outside to the mercy of the harsh cold and the violent winds. Throughout the long nights he stayed up until after his parents had gone to sleep. Then he would open a wooden chest and take out of it the book of the Gospels to read from it in secret by the feeble glow of a lamp, looking stealthily from time to time in the direction of his slumbering father, who had forbidden him to read the Book. It was forbidden because the priests did not allow the simple in mind to probe the secrets of the teachings of Jesus. If they did so, then the church would excommunicate them. Thus did Yuhanna pass the days of his youth between that field of wonder and beauty and the book of Jesus, filled with the light and the spirit. Whenever his father spoke he remained silent and in thought, listening to him, but never a word would he utter. Ofttimes he would sit with companions of his own age, silent and

52

looking beyond them to where the evening twilight met the blue of the sky. Whenever he went to church he returned with a feeling of sorrow because the teachings that he heard from the pulpit and altar were not those that he read about in the Gospel. And the life led by the faithful and their leaders was not the beautiful life of which Jesus of Nazareth spoke in His book.

Spring returned to the fields and the meadows, and the snows melted away. On the mountaintops some snow still remained until it in turn melted and ran down the mountainsides and became streams twisting and winding in the valleys below. Soon they met and joined one another until they were swift-flowing rivers, their roaring announcing to all that Nature had awakened from her sleep. The apple and the walnut trees blossomed and the poplar and the willow bore new leaves; and on the heights appeared grass and flowers. Yuhanna grew weary of his existence by the fireside; his calves fretted in their narrow enclosure and hungered for the green pastures, for their store

53

of barley and straw was almost consumed. So he set them free of their manger and led them out to the countryside. He carried his Bible under his cloak so that nobody should see it, until he reached the meadow that rested on the shoulder of the valley near the fields of a monastery which stood up grimly like a tower in the midst of the hillocks.[1] There his calves dispersed to pasture on the grass. Yuhanna sat him down against a rock, now looking across the valley in all its beauty, now reading the words in his book that spoke to him of the Kingdom of Heaven.

It was a day toward the end of Lent, when the villagers, who were abstaining from the eating of meats, awaited impatiently the coming of Easter. But Yuhanna, like all the poor farmers, knew no difference between days of fasting and days of feasting; to him life itself was one long fast-day. His food was never more than bread kneaded with the sweat of his brow and fruits purchased with his heart's blood. For him

---

[1] This is a wealthy monastery in North Lebanon, owning extensive lands. It is known as the Deir Elisha Al-Nabi (i.e., Monastery of the Prophet Elisha). — Author's note.

54

abstention from meats and rich foods was a natural thing. Fasting brought him not hunger of the body but hunger of the spirit; for it brought to him the sorrow of the Son of Man and the close of His life upon earth.

Around Yuhanna the birds fluttered, calling out one to another, and flocks of doves flew swiftly overhead; the flowers swayed gently to and fro in the breeze as though bathing themselves in the warming rays of the sun. He read the while, immersed in his book, and then lifted up his head. He saw the church domes in the towns and villages scattered around the valley and heard the pealing of the bells. He closed his eyes and let his spirit soar high across the centuries to old Jerusalem, there to follow in the footsteps of Jesus in the streets, inquiring of the passers-by about Him. They answered and said: "Here did He cure the blind and make the halt to rise. There did they make for Him a crown of thorns and place it upon His head. In this street He stopped and addressed the crowd in parables. In that place they bound Him to a pillar and spat in His face and whipped Him. In this lane did He forgive the harlot her sins. Yonder fell He to the ground under the weight of His cross."

The hours passed, the while Yuhanna suffered with the God-man in agony of body and was exalted with Him in spirit. When he rose from his place the midday sun was high. He looked around him but did not see his calves; he sought them everywhere, perplexed at their disappearance in those flat meadows. When he reached the road that wound across the fields like lines on the palm of a hand, he saw from afar a man clothed in black standing in the midst of the gardens. He hastened toward him and on drawing near perceived that it was one of the monks from the monastery. Yuhanna bowed his head in greeting and asked him if he had seen his calves in the gardens.

The monk, trying to conceal his anger, looked at him and answered roughly: "Yes, I have seen them, they are yonder; come, and thou shalt see them." Yuhanna followed the monk until they came to the monastery. There he saw his calves tethered by ropes within a wide enclosure and guarded by another monk.

In his hand was a heavy stick with which he belabored the beasts whenever they moved. When Yuhanna made as if to lead them away, the monk seized him by his cloak and, turning in the direction of the doorway of the monastery, shouted in a loud voice: "Here is the guilty shepherd boy; I have caught him." At his cry priests and monks ran from all directions toward him, led by their Superior, a man distinguished from his companions by his dress of fine material and his soured features. They surrounded Yuhanna like soldiers scrambling after loot. He looked at the Superior and in a gentle voice said: "What have I done that you call me a criminal and why have you seized me?" The Superior answered him in a voice that rasped like a saw: "Thou hast pastured these cattle on land that is the monastery's land and they have nibbled and gnawed at our vines. We have seized them because the shepherd is responsible for the damage wrought by his flock." His angry face grew hard as he spoke. Then spoke Yuhanna with pleading in his voice: "Father," he said, "they are but dumb creatures without intelligence, and I am a poor man and possess naught except the strength of my forearm and these beasts. Let me take them away and I shall promise not to come to these meadows again."

The Father Superior moved a step forward, raised his hand toward the heavens, and again spoke: "God has put us in this place and He has entrusted to us the guardianship of this land, the land of His chosen, the great Elisha. Day and night do we guard it with all our might, for it is sacred; those who approach it will it consume with fire. If thou refusest to render account to the monastery, then shall the very grass turn to poison in the bellies of thy beasts. There is no escape for thee for we shall keep the calves here in our enclosure until thou hast paid the last fils."[1]

The Superior was about to go when Yuhanna stopped him and said in a voice of supplication: "I entreat you, my lord, for the sake of these sacred days wherein Jesus suffered and Mary wept in sorrow, to let me go with my calves. Harden not your heart against me; I am poor and the monastery is rich and powerful. It will

---

[1] Coin of fractional value.

assuredly forgive my foolishness and have pity upon my father's years." The Superior looked at him, mocking, and said: "The monastery will not excuse thee, not even to the amount of one grain, stupid one; it matters not whether thou be rich or poor. Who art thou to adjure me by things sacred since it is we alone that know their secrets and hidden things? If thou wouldst take away the calves from these pastures, then shalt thou redeem them in the sum of three dinars to pay for what they have consumed of the crops." Said Yuhanna in a choking voice: "I have nothing, father, not even a para piece. Have compassion on me and my poverty."

The Superior caressed his thick beard with his fingers. "Then go thou and sell part of thy field and return with three dinars. Is it not better for thee to enter heaven and possess no field than to earn Elisha's wrath with thy ceaseless arguing before his altar and thus go down into hell, where all is eternal fire?"

Yuhanna remained silent for a while. From his eyes shone a light and his features expanded with joy. His bearing changed from one of entreaty and pleading to one of strength and re-

solve. When he spoke it was in a voice in which
were knowledge and the determination of
youth:

"Must the poor sell the fields that earn them
their bread and maintain their existence in order to fill further the coffers of the monastery,
heavy with gold and silver? Is it just that the
poor should be yet poorer and the wretched die
of hunger that great Elisha may forgive the sins
of hungry beasts? " The Superior shook his
head haughtily. "Jesus the Christ said: For unto
everyone that hath shall be given and he shall
have abundance; but from him that hath not
shall be taken away even that which he hath."

As Yuhanna heard these words his heart beat
faster in his breast, he grew in spirit and in-
creased in stature. It was as though the earth
were developing at his feet. From his pocket he
drew out his Bible as the warrior draws his
sword to defend himself, and cried: "Thus do
you make a mockery of the teachings of this
Book, O hypocrites, and use that which is most
sacred in life to spread the evils therein. Woe to
you when the Son of Man shall come a second
time and lay in ruins your monasteries and scat-

ter their stones across the valley and burn with fire your altars and images! Woe to you by the innocent blood of Jesus and the tears of His mother's weeping, for they shall overwhelm you as a flood and carry you down to the depths of the abyss! Woe to you who prostrate yourselves before the idols of your greed and conceal beneath your black raiment the blackness of your deeds! Woe to you who move your lips in prayer while your hearts are yet hard as rock; who bend low in humility before the altar yet in your souls rebel against your God! In your harshness you have brought me to this place and seized hold of me as a transgressor for the sake of a little pasture land that the sun has nourished for us equally. When I entreat you in the name of Jesus and adjure you by the days of His sorrow and pain, you scoff at me as one who speaks in ignorance. Take then this Book, look into it, and show me when Jesus was not forgiving. Read this divine tragedy and tell me where He speaks without mercy and compassion. Was it in His Sermon on the Mount or in His teachings in the temple before the persecutors of the wretched harlot or upon Golgotha as He opened

61

wide His arms on the cross to embrace all mankind? Look down, all you hard of heart, upon these poor towns and villages in whose dwellings the sick writhe in agony on beds of pain; in whose prisons the unfortunate pass their days in despair; at whose gates the beggars beg; on whose highways the stranger makes his bed, and in whose cemeteries the widow and the orphan weep. But you are here living in sloth and idleness and comfort, enjoying the yield of the fields and the grapes of the vine. You visit not the sick and the imprisoned; nor do you feed the hungry or give refuge to the stranger or comfort to the mourner. Would that you were content with what you hold and that which you have plundered from our forefathers! You stretch out your hands as the viper its head and rob the widow of the labor of her hands and the peasant of his store against old age."

Yuhanna ceased from talking in order to regain his breath. Then he went on, his head lifted proudly and said in a gentle voice:

"You are many and I am one. Do to me as you wish. The ewe may fall as prey to the wolves in the darkness of the night, but her blood will stain the stones of the valley until the coming of dawn and the rising of the sun."

Yuhanna spoke these words, and in his voice was a strength inspired, a force that restrained the monks from all movement and caused anger and harshness to rise within them. They trembled in their rage and ground their teeth like caged and hungry lions, awaiting a sign from their chief to tear the youth to pieces. So they were until Yuhanna had ceased speaking and became silent like the calm after the storm has wrought destruction on the topmost branches of a tree and the strongest of plants. Then cried the Superior: "Seize this miserable sinner; take from him the Book and drag him away to a dark cell. Those who would curse God's elect shall receive pardon neither here nor in the hereafter." The monks fell upon Yuhanna as the lion falls upon his prey; they pinioned his arms and led him away to a narrow chamber. Before locking the door on him they belabored his body with blows and kicks.

In that dark place stood Yuhanna, the victor whom fortune has given to the foe as captive. Through a small opening in the wall he looked out on the valley reposing in the sunlight. His face became illumined and his spirit felt the embrace of a divine content; a sweet tranquillity took possession of him. The narrow cell imprisoned his body, but his spirit was free to roam with the breeze among the meadows and ruins. The hands of the monks had bruised his limbs, but they had not touched his inmost feelings; in those he rested in safety with Jesus the Nazarene. Persecution harms not the just man nor does oppression destroy one who is on the side of truth. Socrates drank of the hemlock smiling; Paul was stoned rejoicing. When we oppose the hidden conscience, it does us hurt. When we betray it, it judges us.

The parents of Yuhanna came to know of what had befallen their only child. His mother came to the monastery walking with the aid of her stick and threw herself at the feet of the Superior. She wept and kissed his hands and beseeched him to have pity on her son and pardon his ignorance. The Superior lifted his eyes heavenwards like one raised above worldly affairs and said to the woman: "We can forgive the playfulness of thy son and show tolerance toward his foolishness, but the monastery possesses sacred rights to which account must be rendered. We in our humility forgive the transgressions of men, but great Elisha forgives not nor pardons the trespassers on his vineyards and those who put to pasture their beasts on his land."

The mother looked up at him while the tears ran down her withered old cheeks. Then from around her neck she took a silver collar and put it in his hand, saying: "I have naught except this collar, father. It is a gift of my mother, given me on the day of my marriage. Perchance the monastery will accept it as an atonement for the guilt of my only son."

The Superior took the collar and put it in his pocket and addressed the mother, the while she kissed his hands in gratitude and thankfulness: "Woe to this generation, for the verses of the Book have become contrariwise and the children have eaten of sour grapes and the fathers' teeth are set on edge! Go now, good woman, and pray for thy foolish son that Heaven may cure him and give back his reason."

Yuhanna went out from his prison and walked

slowly before his calves by the side of his mother as she leaned on her staff, bowed down under the weight of her years. When he reached the hut, he left the calves to browse and sat beside the window in silence, looking at the fading light of day. After a little time he heard his father whisper these words into his mother's ear: "Many times have I told thee, Sarah, that our son is weak in mind, but never didst thou agree with me. Now thou dost no longer contradict me, for his actions have justified my words. What the reverend father told thee today have I been telling thee for years."

Yuhanna remained looking toward the west, where the rays of the setting sun put color to the close-packed masses of cloud.

II

It was Easter-tide and fasting gave place to feasting. The building of the new church was completed and it rose above the houses of Besharry, in whose midst it stood, like the palace of a prince among the mean dwellings of his subjects. The people stood and watched for the coming of the bishop to dedicate their sanctuary and consecrate its altars. And when they felt that the time of his arrival was near they went out from the town in processions and he entered with them to songs of praise from the young men and the chanting of the priests, and the clashing of cymbals and ringing of bells. When he dismounted from his horse, adorned with decorated saddle and silver bridle, he was met by men of religion and notable persons who welcomed him with pomp and fitting words and verse and songs of praise. When he reached the new church he was invested with a priestly robe

67

embroidered in gold, and a jewel-encrusted crown was put upon his head. Then he was girded with the shepherd's crook of cunning workmanship and precious stones. He made a circuit of the church, singing and chanting orisons with the priests, while around him rose and swirled goodly-smelling incense and the flickering flames of many candles.

At that hour Yuhanna was standing among the shepherds and tillers of the soil on a raised platform observing this spectacle through his sad eyes. He sighed bitterly in his pain and grief as he saw on the one side silken clothes and gold vessels, censers and costly silver lamps; and on the other, crowds of poor and wretched people who had come up from little villages and hamlets to assist at the rejoicings of this festival and the ceremony of consecration. On the one side, power in its velvets and satins; on the other, misery in its rags and tatters. Here wealth and power personifying the religion with its songs and chants; there an enfeebled people, humble and poor, rejoicing in its secret soul in the Resurrection. Praying in silence and sighing sighs that rose from the bottom of broken hearts to

float on the ether and whisper into the ears of the air. Here the leaders and headmen to whom power gave life like the life of the evergreen cypress tree. There the peasants who submit, whose existence is a ship with Death for its captain; whose rudder is broken by the waves and whose sails are torn by the winds; now rising, now sinking between the anger of the deep and the terror of the storm. Here harsh tyranny; there blind obedience. Which one is parent to the other? Is tyranny a strong tree that grows not except on low ground? Or is submission an abandoned field in which naught lives but thorns?

With these sorrowful reflections and torturing thoughts did Yuhanna occupy himself. He pressed his arms against his breast as if his throat were closing in upon his breathing, in fear that his breast were being rent asunder to let go his breath. In this manner he remained until the ceremony of dedication was at an end, when the people dispersed and went their diverse ways.

Soon he began to feel as though there were a spirit in the air urging him to arise and speak in its name; and in the crowd a power moving him

69

to come forth as a preacher before heaven and earth.

He came to the end of the platform and, lifting up his eyes, made a sign with his hand to the heavens. In a strong voice that compelled the ears and eyes to give attention he cried:

"Behold thou, O Jesus, Man of Nazareth, who sittest within the circle of light on high. Look down from beyond the blue dome of heaven upon this earth; whose elements Thou didst wear yesterday as a cloak. Look, O faithful Tiller, for the thorns of the thicket have strangled the flowers whose seeds did quicken into life by the sweat of Thy brow. Look, O good Shepherd, for the weak lamb Thou didst carry on Thy shoulder is torn to pieces by wild beasts. Thine innocent blood is sucked into the earth, and Thy hot tears are dried up in the hearts of men. The warmth of Thy breath is scattered before desert winds. This field hallowed by Thy feet is become a battleground where the feet of the strong grind the ribs of the outcast, where the hand of the oppressor blights the spirit of the weak. The persecuted cry out from the darkness, and those who sit upon thrones in Thy name heed not their cries. Neither is the weeping of the bereaved heard by those who preach Thy words from pulpits. The lamb that Thou didst send for the sake of the Lord of Life is become a rampaging beast tearing to pieces the wings of the Lamb enfolded by Thine arms. The word of life that Thou didst bring down from the heart of God is concealed and hidden within the pages of books, and in its place is a terrible shouting, putting fear and dread into all hearts. These people, O Jesus, have raised temples and tabernacles to the glory of Thy name and adorned them with woven silk and molten gold. They have left naked the bodies of Thy chosen poor in the cold streets: yet do they fill the air with the smoke of incense and candles. Those who believe in Thy godlike state have they robbed of bread. Though the air echoes to their psalms and hymns, yet they hear not the orphan's cry, neither the widow's lamentation. Come then, O Jesus, a second time, and drive out from the temple those who trade in religion, for they have made of it a nest of vipers with their cunning and guile. Come, and do reckoning with

71

these Cæsars who have wrested from the weak that which is theirs and God's. Behold the vine that Thy right hand did plant. The worms have eaten of its shoots, and its grapes are trampled beneath the feet of the passer-by. Consider those upon whom Thou didst enjoin peace and see how they are divided, contending among themselves. Our troubled souls and oppressed hearts have they made as victims of their wars. On their feast-days and holy days they lift up their voices saying glory to God in His heaven, peace upon earth, and joy to all men. Is Thy heavenly Father glorified when corrupt lips and lying tongues utter His name? Is there peace upon earth when the children of sorrow toil in the fields and see their strength ebbing away in the light of the sun to feed the mouth of the strong and fill the tyrant's belly? Is there rejoicing among men when the outcast look with their broken eyes toward death as the conquered looks to his deliverer? What is peace, gentle Jesus? Is it in the eyes of children at the breasts of hungry mothers in cold dark dwellings? Or in the bodies of the needy who sleep in their beds of stone wishing for the food that comes not to them but is thrown by the priests to their fattened swine? What is joy, O Jesus? Does it exist when a prince can buy the strength of men and the honor of women for a few pieces of silver? Is it in those silent ones that are slaves in body and soul to whosoever dazzles their eyes with the gleam of bejeweled orders and the flash of stones in rings and the silk of their garments? Is there rejoicing in the cries of the oppressed and downtrodden when tyrants fall upon them with the sword and crush the bodies of their women and young ones under horses' hoofs and make drunk the earth with their blood? Stretch forth Thy strong hand, Jesus, and save us, for the oppressor's hand is heavy upon us. Or send to us Death, that he might lead us to the grave, wherein we shall sleep in peace against the second coming, secure in the shadow of Thy cross. For verily our life is naught but a darkness whose inhabitants are evil spirits, and a valley wherein snakes and dragons make sport. What are our days except whetted swords concealed by night between our bed-coverings and revealed by the morning light hanging over our heads whenever the love of existence leads us

73

to the fields? Have mercy, O Jesus, on these multitudes joined together as one by Thy name on the day of the Resurrection. Have compassion on their weakness and humility."

Thus did Yuhanna hold converse with the heavens while the people stood around him. Some were pleased and praised him; others were angry and reviled him. One shouted: "He says aright and speaks for us before Heaven, for we are oppressed." Another said: "He is possessed and speaks with the tongue of an evil spirit." That one cried: "We never heard such foolishness from our fathers before us; neither do we wish to hear it now." Yet another whispered into his neighbor's ear, saying: "At the sound of his voice I felt within me an awful trembling that shook my very heart, for he spoke with a strange power." Answered his friend: "It is so; but our leaders are more knowledgeable in these affairs than are we. It is wrong to doubt them."

As the cries rose from all sides and swelled into a roar like the sea only to be scattered and lost in the ether, a priest appeared, seized hold of Yuhanna, and delivered him up to the police. They led him away to the Governor's house.

74

When they asked him questions he answered not a word, for he remembered that Jesus was silent too before His persecutors. So they threw him into the dark prison house and there he slept, gently leaning against the stone wall.

And on the morning of the following day came Yuhanna's father to testify before the Governor to his son's madness.

"My lord," he said, "often have I heard him babbling in his solitude and talking of strange things that have no existence. Night after night has he spoken into the silence in unknown words, calling upon the shadows of darkness in a terrible voice like that of sorcerers uttering incantations. Ask of the boys of the quarter who used to sit with him, for they know how his mind was attracted by another world beyond. When they spoke to him, seldom did he answer. And when he did speak, his words were confused and without relation to their conversation. Ask of his mother, for more than all others was she aware of a soul stripped of all its senses. Ofttimes did she see him looking toward the horizon with eyes staring and glazed, and hear him speaking with passion of the trees and brooks and flowers and stars in the way children prattle of trifles. Ask of the monks in the monastery with whom he contended yesterday, mocking at their godliness and scorning their sacred way of life. He is mad, my lord, but to his mother and me he is kind. He sustains us in our old age and fulfills our wants with the sweat of his brow. Show him mercy through your compassion upon us and forgive his foolishness for the sake of his parents."

Yuhanna was set free and the story of his madness spread abroad. The young men spoke of him with mocking. But the maidens looked at him with sad eyes and said: "For much that is strange in men are the heavens accountable. So in this youth is beauty united with madness, and the light of his beautiful eyes wedded to the darkness of his sick soul."

Between the meadows and the heights, clothed in their garments of flowers and plants, sat Yuhanna by the calves, who had fled from the stress and strife of men to the good pastures. He looked with tear-dimmed eyes toward the villages and hamlets scattered upon the shoulders of the valley and, sighing deeply, repeated these words:

"You are many and I am one. Say what you will of me and do to me as you wish. The ewe may fall as prey to the wolves in the darkness of the night, but her blood will stain the stones of the valley until the coming of the dawn and the rising of the sun."

A NOTE ON THE AUTHOR

Kahlil Gibran, poet, philosopher, and artist, was born in 1883 into an affluent and musical Lebanese family. He was a college student in Syria at the age of fifteen, studied art in Paris at the Ecole des Beaux Arts, and had visited America twice before he came to New York to stay in 1912 and adopted English as his literary language. He died in New York City's Greenwich Village on April 10, 1931.

His drawings and paintings have been exhibited in the great capitals of the world and were compared by Auguste Rodin to the work of William Blake. The Prophet, his most popular book, published in 1923, has been translated into more than twenty languages, and has sold well over six million copies in this country alone.

A NOTE ON THE TYPE USED

This book has been set in a modern Linotype adaptation of a type designed by William Caslon, the first (1692–1766), greatest of English letter founders. The Caslon face, an artistic, easily read type, has had two centuries of ever increasing popularity in our own country—it is of interest to note that the first copies of the Declaration of Independence and the first paper currency distributed to the citizens of the new-born nation were printed in this type face.

PRINTED AND BOUND BY THE BOOK PRESS,
BRATTLEBORO, VERMONT